JAN 13

An Illustrated Timeline of
U.S. PRESIDENTS

by Mary Englar

illustrated by Len Epstein

PICTURE WINDOW BOOKS
a capstone imprint

Special thanks to our adviser, Terry Flaherty, PhD, Professor of English,
Minnesota State University, Mankato, for his expertise.

Editor: Shelly Lyons
Designer: Lori Bye
Art Director: Nathan Gassman
Production Specialist: Danielle Ceminsky
The illustrations in this book were created with pencil and digital color.

Photo Credits: Shutterstock: J. Helgason, Tischenko Irina

Picture Window Books
1710 Roe Crest Drive
North Mankato, MN 56003
877-845-8392
www.capstonepub.com

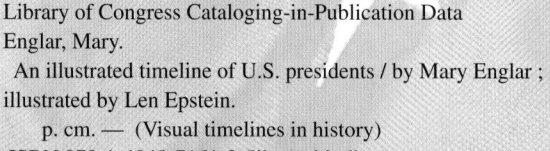
All books published by Picture Window Books
are manufactured with paper containing at least
10 percent post-consumer waste.

Library of Congress Cataloging-in-Publication Data
Englar, Mary.
 An illustrated timeline of U.S. presidents / by Mary Englar ;
illustrated by Len Epstein.
    p. cm. — (Visual timelines in history)
 ISBN 978-1-4048-7161-8 (library binding)
 ISBN 978-1-4048-7254-7 (paperback)
 1. Presidents—United States—History—Chronology—Juvenile
literature. 2. United States—History—Chronology—Juvenile literature.
3. United States—Politics and government—Chronology—Juvenile
literature. I. Epstein, Len, ill. II. Title.
 E176.1.E49 2012
 973.09'9—dc23

                        2011028889

Printed in the United States of America in North Mankato, Minnesota.
102011   006405CGS12

How many men have been president of the United States? Which president served the longest in office? Which president served only one month? This timeline book is your guide to the 44 presidents of the United States—when they were born, when they died, and some other cool facts too! You'll also find out about wars and other key events in the country's history. Start from the beginning of the timeline, or skip around. This book is divided into dates and chapters, so it's easy to jump from one page to another.

A NEW NATION IS BORN

1st President
George Washington (1789–1797)

Birth: February 22, 1732, Pope's Creek, Virginia
Death: December 14, 1799, Mount Vernon, Virginia
Political Party: Federalist
Fast Fact: Washington has several dentures made of animal teeth, human teeth, lead, and ivory.

April 19, 1775
The Revolutionary War between the United States and Great Britain begins.

July 4, 1776
The Declaration of Independence is approved. The United States declares itself independent from Great Britain.

September 3, 1783
The Revolutionary War ends with the Treaty of Paris. The United States wins its independence.

1790
U.S. leaders choose land near the Potomac River as the site for the capital city. It will be called Washington, D.C.

3rd President
Thomas Jefferson (1801–1809)

Birth: April 13, 1743, Shadwell Plantation, Virginia
Death: July 4, 1826, Monticello, Virginia
Political Party: Democratic-Republican
Fast Fact: Jefferson dies on the 50th anniversary of the Declaration of Independence. It's the same day John Adams passes away.

December 15, 1791
The Bill of Rights becomes part of the U.S. Constitution. It protects the rights of all Americans.

April 30, 1803
The United States makes the Louisiana Purchase from France. The deal doubles the size of the United States.

2nd President
John Adams (1797–1801)

Birth: October 30, 1735, Braintree (now Quincy), Massachusetts
Death: July 4, 1826, Quincy, Massachusetts
Political Party: Federalist
Fast Fact: Adams is the first president to live in the White House. But it has only six finished rooms.

WAR AND GROWTH

4th President
James Madison (1809–1817)

Birth: March 16, 1751, Port Conway, Virginia
Death: June 28, 1836, Montpelier, Virginia
Political Party: Democratic-Republican
Fast Fact: Madison is the first president to wear long pants. Other presidents before him wore knee-length pants.

Virginia

June 18, 1812

The United States declares war on Great Britain, starting the War of 1812.

February 17, 1815

The War of 1812 ends when the United States formally approves the Treaty of Ghent.

5th President
James Monroe (1817–1825)

Birth: April 28, 1758, Westmoreland County, Virginia
Death: July 4, 1831, New York, New York
Political Party: Democratic-Republican
Fast Fact: Upon leaving office, Monroe is deeply in debt. Eventually he moves in with his daughter.

6th President
John Quincy Adams (1825–1829)

Birth: July 11, 1767, Braintree
(now Quincy), Massachusetts
Death: February 23, 1848, Washington, D.C.
Political Party: Federalist; Democratic-
Republican; Whig
Fast Fact: In 1843, Adams is the first former
president to be photographed.

1830
John Quincy Adams is elected to the House of
Representatives. He becomes the first former
president to serve in Congress.

December 2, 1823
President Monroe introduces the
Monroe Doctrine. It says that North
and South America are not to be
taken over by other countries.

7th President
Andrew Jackson (1829–1837)

Birth: March 15, 1767, Waxhaw area,
North Carolina/South Carolina border
Death: June 8, 1845, Nashville, Tennessee
Political Party: Democrat
Fast Fact: Jackson has a pet parrot named
Poll. The bird can talk, but it sometimes
says curse words.

7

A GROWING NATION

8th President
Martin Van Buren (1837–1841)

Birth: December 5, 1782, Kinderhook, New York
Death: July 24, 1862, Kinderhook, New York
Political Party: Democrat
Fast Fact: When Van Buren runs for president, Old Kinderhook clubs from his hometown support him. Old Kinderhook is later shortened to "OK," which we use today for "all right."

1838
In a march known as the Trail of Tears, the Cherokee nation is forced to move from its homeland. The people walk from southeastern parts of the United States to present-day Oklahoma.

April 4, 1841
President Harrison dies of pneumonia. He's the first president to die in office.

9th President
William Henry Harrison
(March 4, 1841–April 4, 1841)

Birth: February 9, 1773, Berkeley Plantation, Virginia
Death: April 4, 1841, Washington, D.C.
Political Party: Whig
Fast Fact: Harrison serves just 32 days in office. That's the shortest amount of time any president has served.

10th President
John Tyler (1841–1845)

Birth: March 29, 1790, Charles City County, Virginia

Death: January 18, 1862, Richmond, Virginia

Political Party: Democrat; Whig

Fast Fact: Tyler has a pet canary named Johnny Ty.

April 25, 1846
Mexicans attack American troops in Texas. The Mexican-American War begins.

January 24, 1848
The Gold Rush starts when James Marshall finds gold in modern-day California.

11th President
James K. Polk (1845–1849)

Birth: November 2, 1795, Mecklenburg County, North Carolina

Death: June 15, 1849, Nashville, Tennessee

Political Party: Democrat

Fast Fact: During Polk's presidency, the United States grows by more than 1,000,000 square miles (2,600,000 square kilometers)! The country adds all or part of 11 current states.

1,000,000 Square Miles

THE FIRST WHITE HOUSE LIBRARY

12th President

Zachary Taylor (1849-1850)

Birth: November 24, 1784, Orange County, Virginia
Death: July 9, 1850, Washington, D.C.
Political Party: Whig
Fast Fact: Prior to 1848, Taylor had never voted in a presidential election.

Ballot Box

July 9, 1850
President Taylor dies unexpectedly, possibly of cholera.

13th President

Millard Fillmore (1850-1853)

Birth: January 7, 1800, Summerhill, New York
Death: March 8, 1874, Buffalo, New York
Political Party: Whig
Fast Fact: Fillmore and his wife, Abigail, create the first permanent library in the White House.

14th President
Franklin Pierce (1853–1857)

Birth: November 23, 1804, Hillsboro, New Hampshire
Death: October 8, 1869, Concord, New Hampshire
Political Party: Democrat
Fast Fact: Pierce has a strong religious faith. He refuses to do any work on Sundays. He doesn't even open and read his mail.

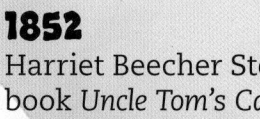

1852
Harriet Beecher Stowe's book *Uncle Tom's Cabin* is published. It helps spark the movement to end slavery in the United States.

A DIVIDED NATION

15th President
James Buchanan (1857–1861)

Birth: April 23, 1791,
Cove Gap, Pennsylvania
Death: June 1, 1868, near
Lancaster, Pennsylvania
Political Party: Democrat
Fast Fact: Buchanan is the
only president who never marries.

April 12, 1861
The Battle of Fort Sumter, near
Charleston, South Carolina, begins.
It marks the beginning of the
Civil War.

December 20, 1860
South Carolina removes itself from
the United States. Ten other southern
states soon follow. They become the
Confederate States of America.

16th President
Abraham Lincoln (1861–1865)

Birth: February 12, 1809, near Hardin
(now Larue) County, Kentucky
Death: April 15, 1865, Washington, D.C.
Political Party: Whig; Republican
Fast Fact: Lincoln is the first president born
outside the original 13 states.

Kentucky

April 9, 1865
Confederate General Robert E. Lee surrenders to Union forces. The Civil War is over.

April 14, 1865
President Lincoln is shot by John Wilkes Booth. He is the first president to be assassinated while in office.

January 1, 1863
President Lincoln issues the Emancipation Proclamation. It says slaves in the Confederate States now have freedom.

17th President
Andrew Johnson (1865–1869)

Birth: December 29, 1808, Raleigh, North Carolina
Death: July 31, 1875, Carter's Station, Tennessee
Political Party: Democrat; Unionist
Fast Fact: Johnson never attends school, but he teaches himself to read. His wife, Eliza McCardle, helps him learn reading, writing, and math.

A GREAT FIRE

18th President

(Hiram) Ulysses S. Grant (1869–1877)

Birth: April 27, 1822, Point Pleasant, Ohio
Death: July 23, 1885, Mount McGregor, New York
Political Party: Republican
Fast Fact: Grant loves horses. He once got a speeding ticket for riding his horse too fast.

Speed Limit
3 Mi. per H...

October 8, 1871
The Great Chicago Fire begins burning near downtown Chicago. It burns for more than 24 hours. About 100,000 people lose their homes.

19th President

Rutherford B. Hayes (1877–1881)

Birth: October 4, 1822, Delaware, Ohio
Death: January 17, 1893, Fremont, Ohio
Political Party: Republican
Fast Fact: Hayes was a highly respected Union general in the Civil War.

20th President

James A. Garfield (1881)

Birth: November 19, 1831,
Orange Township, Ohio
Death: September 19, 1881,
Elberon, New Jersey
Political Party: Republican
Fast Fact: Garfield is the first
left-handed president.

July 2, 1881
President Garfield is shot by an
unhappy citizen. Garfield dies two
months later from an infection.

21st President

Chester A. Arthur (1881–1885)

Birth: October 5, 1829,
Fairfield, Vermont
Death: November 18, 1886,
New York, New York
Political Party: Republican
Fast Fact: Arthur loves clothes and
has more than 80 pairs of pants. He
is nicknamed "Elegant Arthur."

July 4, 1884
As a gift of friendship, France
presents the United States
with the Statue of Liberty.

ONE PRESIDENT, TWO TERMS

23rd President
Benjamin Harrison (1889–1893)

Birth: August 20, 1833, North Bend, Ohio
Death: March 13, 1901, Indianapolis, Indiana
Political Party: Republican
Fast Fact: Harrison is the first president to have electric lights in the White House. After he receives a shock, his family is afraid to touch them.

22nd President
(Stephen) Grover Cleveland (1885–1889)

Birth: March 18, 1837, Caldwell, New Jersey
Death: June 24, 1908, Princeton, New Jersey
Political Party: Democrat
Fast Fact: Cleveland is the only president to be elected to two terms, four years apart.

24th President
(Stephen) Grover Cleveland (1893–1897)

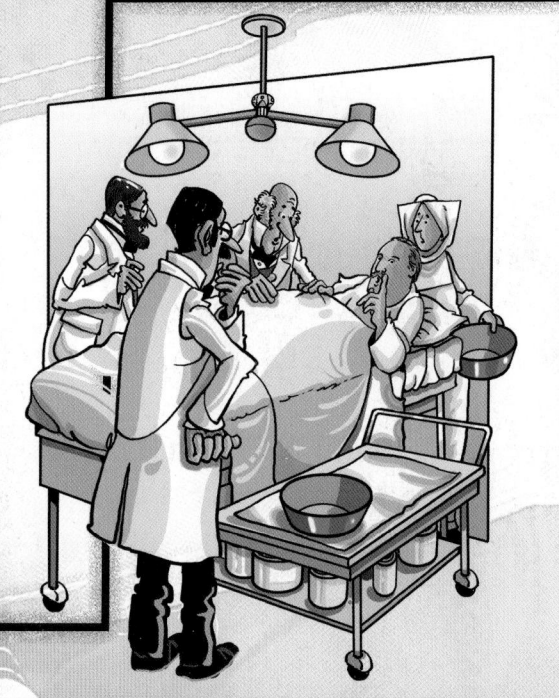

Birth: March 18, 1837, Caldwell, New Jersey
Death: June 24, 1908, Princeton, New Jersey
Political Party: Democrat
Fast Fact: Cleveland has a secret surgery to remove a growth in his jaw. Doctors give him a rubber jaw.

December 10, 1898

Spain signs the Treaty of Paris. The treaty gives the United States control over Cuba, Guam, Puerto Rico, and the Philippines. The Spanish-American War ends.

April 25, 1898

The United States and Spain enter into war over Cuba's independence. In July, Spanish troops surrender to U.S. forces.

September 6, 1901

President McKinley is shot twice while in Buffalo, New York. He dies eight days later.

25th President
William McKinley (1897–1901)

Birth: January 29, 1843, Niles, Ohio
Death: September 14, 1901, Buffalo, New York
Political Party: Republican
Fast Fact: In the late 1890s, a supporter of McKinley names a mountain in Alaska after the president.

Mt. McKinley

WORLD WAR I BEGINS

▶ 26th President
Theodore Roosevelt (1901–1909)

Birth: October 27, 1858, New York, New York
Death: January 6, 1919, Oyster Bay, New York
Political Party: Republican
Fast Fact: Roosevelt is the first president to have a telephone in his home.

October 1, 1908
The Ford Motor Company makes the first car the U.S. public will use widely. It's called the Model T.

27th President
William Howard Taft (1909–1913)

Birth: September 15, 1857, Cincinnati, Ohio
Death: March 8, 1930, Washington, D.C.
Political Party: Republican
Fast Fact: After serving as president, Taft is nominated as Chief Justice of the United States in 1921.

28th President
(Thomas) Woodrow Wilson (1913–1921)

Birth: December 28, 1856, Staunton, Virginia
Death: February 3, 1924, Washington, D.C.
Political Party: Democrat
Fast Fact: Wilson shows the first movie in the White House.

April 6, 1917
The United States joins France, Great Britain, and Russia to fight in World War I.

November 11, 1918
Germany surrenders in World War I, and all nations agree to stop fighting.

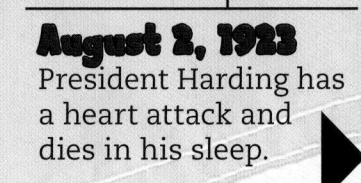

August 2, 1923
President Harding has a heart attack and dies in his sleep.

29th President
Warren G. Harding (1921–1923)

Birth: November 2, 1865, Corsica (now Blooming Grove), Ohio
Death: August 2, 1923, San Francisco, California
Political Party: Republican
Fast Fact: Harding is the first president to own a radio and to make a speech over the radio.

WORLD WAR II BEGINS

30th President
(John) Calvin Coolidge (1923–1929)

Birth: July 4, 1872, Plymouth, Vermont
Death: January 5, 1933, Northampton, Massachusetts
Political Party: Republican
Fast Fact: Coolidge is the only president to be born on Independence Day, July 4.

October 27, 1929
Prices on the New York Stock Exchange crash. The Great Depression begins and will last at least 10 years.

1927
Philo Farnsworth, an American inventor, makes the first fully electronic, black-and-white TV.

31st President
Herbert Hoover (1929–1933)

Birth: August 10, 1874, West Branch, Iowa
Death: October 20, 1964, New York, New York
Political Party: Republican
Fast Fact: Hoover's son, Allan, has two pet alligators. The animals sometimes roam around the White House.

32nd President

Franklin D. Roosevelt (1933–1945)

Birth: January 30, 1882, Hyde Park, New York
Death: April 12, 1945, Warm Springs, Georgia
Political Party: Democrat
Fast Fact: At age 39, Roosevelt catches a virus called polio. The illness causes him to lose all feeling from his waist down.

April 12, 1945
While still in office, President Roosevelt has a stroke in Warm Springs, Georgia. He dies the same day.

June 27, 1950
President Truman sends U.S. troops to Korea. The United States enters the Korean War.

December 7, 1941
Japanese planes bomb U.S. troops at Pearl Harbor, Hawaii. More than 2,000 people are killed. The United States enters into World War II the next day.

August 6 and 9, 1945
The United States bombs the Japanese cities of Hiroshima and Nagasaki. More than 150,000 Japanese citizens die. Japan surrenders, and World War II ends.

33rd President

Harry S. Truman (1945–1953)

Birth: May 8, 1884, Lamar, Missouri
Death: December 26, 1972, Kansas City, Missouri
Political Party: Democrat
Fast Fact: Truman is the first president to give a speech on TV.

FOCUS ON CIVIL RIGHTS

I'm Ike!

I'm Ike!

No, I'm Ike!

I'm Ike!

Whoa, I'm Ike!

He's not Ike, I'm Ike!

34th President

Dwight D. Eisenhower (1953–1961)

Birth: October 14, 1890, Denison, Texas
Death: March 28, 1969, Washington, D.C.
Political Party: Republican
Fast Fact: Eisenhower's nickname is Ike. He has five brothers, and they all share the same nickname at one time or another.

May 1961
President Kennedy sends 400 U.S. troops to Vietnam.

35th President

John F. Kennedy (1961–1963)

Birth: May 29, 1917, Brookline, Massachusetts
Death: November 22, 1963, Dallas, Texas
Political Party: Democrat
Fast Fact: At age 43, Kennedy is the youngest man to be elected president.

Lyndon B. Johnson (1963–1969)

Birth: August 27, 1908, near Johnson City, Texas
Death: January 22, 1973, near Stonewall, Texas
Political Party: Democrat
Fast Fact: Johnson is the first president to fly around the world to visit other countries.

July 2, 1964

The Civil Rights Act is passed. It protects the rights of women and minorities.

November 22, 1963

While riding in a car in Dallas, Texas, President Kennedy is shot by Lee Harvey Oswald. The president dies the same day.

April 4, 1968

Martin Luther King Jr., a civil rights leader, is shot and killed in Memphis, Tennessee.

MOONWALK

37th President
Richard Nixon (1969–1974)

Birth: January 9, 1913, Yorba Linda, California
Death: April 22, 1994, New York, New York
Political Party: Republican
Fast Fact: In July 1969, Nixon phones the crew of Apollo 11 from the White House. The crew has landed on the moon.

July 21, 1969
Neil Armstrong becomes the first man to walk on the moon.

August 8, 1974
President Nixon resigns from office. He is accused of breaking into the Democratic National Committee office in Washington, D.C.

38th President
Gerald Ford (1974–1977)

Birth: July 14, 1913, Omaha, Nebraska
Death: December 26, 2006,
Rancho Mirage, California
Political Party: Republican
Fast Fact: After college, Ford is offered two professional football contracts. But he turns them down to go to law school.

39th President
(James) Jimmy Carter (1977–1981)

Birth: October 1, 1924, Plains, Georgia
Death:
Political Party: Democrat
Fast Fact: Carter is a speed-reader.
He can read 2,000 words per minute.

THE WALL FALLS

40th President
Ronald Reagan (1981–1989)

Birth: February 6, 1911, Tampico, Illinois
Death: June 5, 2004, Los Angeles, California
Political Party: Republican
Fast Fact: Reagan is the first movie actor to be elected president.

November 9, 1989
The Berlin Wall falls. It marks the end of Communist rule over Eastern Europe.

January 17, 1991
The United States invades Iraq. It is the start of Operation Desert Storm.

41st President
George H. W. Bush (1989–1993)

Birth: June 12, 1924, Milton, Massachusetts
Death:
Political Party: Republican
Fast Fact: The U.S. Secret Service's code name for Bush is Timberwolf.

1991

The Soviet Union collapses and is replaced by 15 independent nations.

December 19, 1998

President Clinton becomes the first elected president to be impeached. After going to trial, he is found innocent in February 1999.

August 7, 1998

Terrorists bomb U.S. embassies in Kenya and Tanzania. The bombings kill 224 people.

42nd President

(William) Bill Clinton (1993–2001)

Birth: August 19, 1946, Hope, Arkansas
Death:
Political Party: Democrat
Fast Fact: Clinton names more women and minorities to cabinet positions than any other president before him.

September 11, 2001

Terrorists take control of four U.S. passenger airplanes. Two planes fly into the World Trade Center towers in New York City. The third plane crashes into the Pentagon building in Arlington County, Virginia. The fourth plane crashes in a field in Pennsylvania. Altogether, almost 3,000 people are killed.

October 7, 2001

President Bush announces military action against Afghanistan. It is the start of Operation Enduring Freedom.

Rah

Rah

▶ 43rd President

George W. Bush (2001–2009)

Birth: July 6, 1946, New Haven, Connecticut
Death:
Political Party: Republican
Fast Fact: Bush is the head cheerleader for the football team at his high school, Phillips Academy.

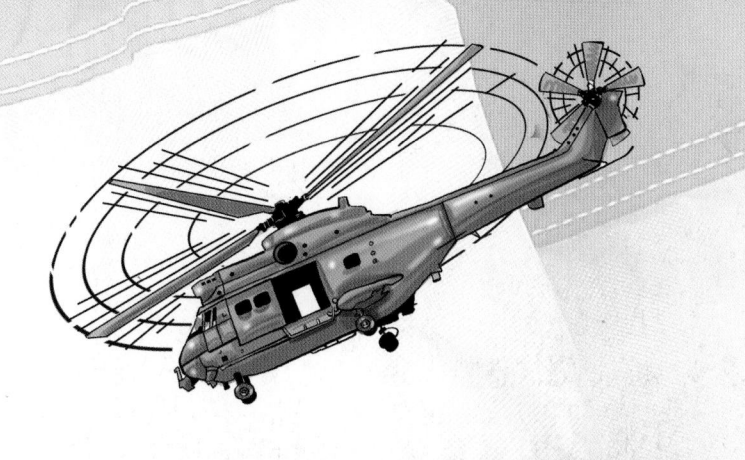

March 10, 2011
The president and first lady host the first White House Conference on Bullying Prevention.

August 2010
President Obama announces an end to Operation Iraqi Freedom.

March 19, 2003
President Bush announces that the United States is at war with Iraq. It is the start of Operation Iraqi Freedom.

44th President
Barack Obama (2009–)

Birth: August 4, 1961, Honolulu, Hawaii
Death:
Political Party: Democrat
Fast Fact: Obama is the first African-American to be elected president.

BUILD YOUR OWN TIMELINE

Think about all of the presidents in our country's history. Pick one and make your own timeline of his life.

Start with the date the president was born, and end with the day the president died. A good source to begin with is www.whitehouse.gov/about/white-house-101/. Ask your librarian to help you find more information.

birth

?

?

death

Glossary

assassinate—to murder an important or famous person

cabinet—a group of officials who give advice to the president

Confederate—a person who supported the cause of the Confederate States of America, or South, during the U.S. Civil War

Congress—the group of people who make the laws for the United States

embassy—a place where representatives of a foreign country live and work

impeach—to bring formal charges of unlawful conduct against a public official

minority—a group that makes up less than half of a large group

resign—to give up a job voluntarily

slavery—the owning of other people; slaves are forced to work without pay

stock—a small part of a company that can be bought or sold

stroke—a problem in the brain causing sudden loss of the ability to feel or move

terrorist—someone who uses violence and threats to frighten people

Union—the United States of America; also the Northern states that fought against the Southern states in the Civil War

TO LEARN MORE

Bausum, Ann. *Our Country's Presidents: All You Need to Know about the Presidents, from George Washington to Barack Obama.* Washington, D.C.: National Geographic, 2009.

Price, Sean Stewart. *U.S. Presidents: Truth and Rumors.* Truth and Rumors. Mankato, Minn.: Capstone Press, 2010.

Wooster, Patricia. *An Illustrated Timeline of U.S. States.* Visual Timelines in History. Mankato, Minn.: Picture Window Books, 2012.

Internet Sites

FactHound offers a safe, fun way to find Internet sites related to this book. All of the sites on FactHound have been researched by our staff.

Here's all you do:

Visit *www.facthound.com*

Type in this code: 9781404871618

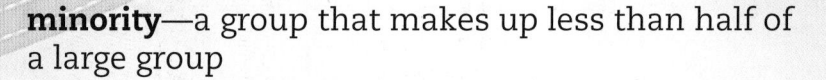

Super-cool stuff!

Check out projects, games and lots more at
www.capstonekids.com

INDEX

Look for all the books in the series:

An Illustrated Timeline of Dinosaurs

An Illustrated Timeline of Inventions and Inventors

An Illustrated Timeline of Space Exploration

An Illustrated Timeline of Transportation

An Illustrated Timeline of U.S. Presidents

An Illustrated Timeline of U.S. States